Enchanted Air

Enchanted Air

TWO CULTURES,
TWO WINGS: A MEMOIR

Margarita Engle

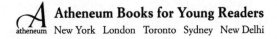 **Atheneum Books for Young Readers**
atheneum New York London Toronto Sydney New Delhi

ATHENEUM BOOKS FOR YOUNG READERS

An imprint of Simon & Schuster Children's Publishing Division

1230 Avenue of the Americas, New York, New York 10020

This work is a memoir. It reflects the author's present recollections of her experiences over a period of years.

Text copyright © 2015 by Margarita Engle

Jacket illustrations, interior illustrations, and hand-lettering copyright © 2015 by Edel Rodriguez

For information about special discounts for bulk purchases, please contact Simon & Schuster Special Sales at 1-866-506-1949 or business@simonandschuster.com.

The Simon & Schuster Speakers Bureau can bring authors to your live event. For more information or to book an event, contact the Simon & Schuster Speakers Bureau at 1-866-248-3049 or visit our website at www.simonspeakers.com.

Book design by Debra Sfetsios-Conover

The text for this book is set in Simoncini Garamond and Trajan Pro.

Manufactured in the United States of America

First Edition

10 9 8 7 6 5 4 3 2 1

Library of Congress Cataloging-in-Publication Data

Engle, Margarita.

Enchanted air : Two cultures, two wings: a memoir / Margarita Engle. — First edition.

pages cm

ISBN 978-1-4814-3522-2

ISBN 978-1-4814-3524-6 (eBook)

1. Engle, Margarita. 2. Cuban Americans—Biography. 3. Women authors, American—20th century—Biography. I. Title.

PS3555.N4254Z46 2015

811'.54—dc23

[B]   2014017408

For my parents, who took me traveling,

and my sister, who shared the adventures,

and for the estimated ten million people

who are currently stateless as the result of

conflicts all over the world

¡Qué fácil es volar, qué fácil es!
Todo consiste en no dejar que el suelo
se acerque a nuestros pies.
Valiente hazaña, ¡el vuelo!, ¡el vuelo!, ¡el vuelo!

How easy it is to fly, how easy!
It's all done by never allowing the ground
to come close to our feet.
Brave deed, flight, flight, flight!

—Antonio Machado, *Poema 53*

❧ CONTENTS ❧

Enchanted Air

Love at First Sight

VALENTINE'S DAY, 1947

Four Years Before I Existed

When my parents met, it was love at first sight. They were standing on the terrace of an art school in an elegant palace now known as the Museo Romántico, the Romantic Museum. They were breathing the enchanted air of Trinidad de Cuba, my mother's hometown. My American father was a visiting artist who had traveled to Trinidad after seeing *National Geographic* magazine photographs of the colonial plaza, where horsemen still galloped along cobblestone streets, beneath soaring church bell towers, against a backdrop of wild green mountains. My mother was a local art student, ready to fall in love.

Since they could not speak the same language, my parents communicated by passing drawings back and forth, like children in the back of a classroom. Their meetings were chaperoned, their conversations mimed—sketches, signs, and gestures had to substitute for words.

He asked her to marry him. Her hands said no. He asked again. Her eyes refused. He packed his suitcase. She rushed to explain, using fingers and facial expressions, that in her old-fashioned town, the rules of romance had been established centuries earlier, at a time when brides were not supposed to seem eager. A marriage proposal must be repeated three times. Saying yes after only two repetitions was my mother's first act of courage.

Magical Travels

1951–1959

FLIGHT

The first time my parents
take me soaring through magical sky
to meet my mother's family in Cuba,
I am so little that I can hardly speak
to my island relatives—
my *abuelita*, my old grandma,
who still loves to dance,
and her ancient *mamá*, my great-grandma,
who still loves to garden, working
just as hard as any strong
young man.

Already, this island is beginning to seem
like a fairy-tale kingdom,
where ordinary people
do impossible
things.

where ordinary
people do imposs.
(cuba)
grandparent

VOICE

Everywhere we go in Cuba,
I hear caged songbirds
and wild parrots.

Somehow, the feathery voices
help me make my decision to sing
instead of speak, and even though
I sing in a voice more froglike
than winged,
I do dare to sing,
and that is what matters
on this island
of bravely dancing,
hardworking
old folks.

MORE LOVE AT FIRST SIGHT

I fall in love with the farm
where my *abuelita*
and her ancient mother
were born.

My dazzled eyes absorb
the lush beauty of a land so wild
and green that the rippling river
on my great-uncle's farm
shimmers like a hummingbird,
all the dangerous crocodiles
and gentle manatees
deeply hidden beneath
quiet waters.

Surely there must be mermaids here,
and talking animals,
the pale, humpbacked Zebu cows
and graceful horses
that roam
peaceful hillsides,
moving as mysteriously
as floating clouds
in the stormy
tropical sky.

LEARNING MANY MEANINGS

The memories that I carry away
from those first visits to the island
are restful.

Cool ceramic floor tiles on a hot day,
and an open-air kitchen with roll-up walls
that are only needed during hurricanes—
when the weather is fine, moths and birds
fly in and out of the house, drifting freely
toward fruit trees in the patio, passing
the old women in rocking chairs,
who fan their faces, welcoming
the sea breeze.

Old women love fresh air, but they are also
afraid of *aires*, a word that can be a whoosh
of refreshing sky-breath, or it can mean
dangerous
spirits.

No Place on the Map

After those first soaring summers,
each time we fly back to our everyday
lives in California, one of my two selves
is left behind: the girl I would be
if we lived on Mami's island
instead of Dad's continent.

On maps, Cuba is crocodile-shaped,
but when I look at a flat paper outline,
I cannot see the beautiful farm
on that crocodile's belly.
I can't find the palm trees,
or bright coral beaches
where flying fish leap,
gleaming
like rainbows.

Sometimes, I feel
like a rolling wave of the sea,
a wave that can only belong
in between
the two solid shores.

Sometimes, I feel
like a bridge,
or a storm.

THE DANCING PLANTS OF CUBA

In California, all the trees and shrubs
stand still, but on the island, coconut palms
and angel's trumpet flowers
love to move around,
dancing.

Fronds and petals wave
in wild wind.
Climbing orchids dangle
from high branches.
The delicate leaflets
of sensitive mimosa plants
coil and curl, folding up
like the pages
of a wizard's book,
each time I touch
their rooted magic.

Maybe I will be a scientist someday,
studying the dancing plants of Cuba.

More and More Meanings

In one country, I hear the sweet words
of another.
Dulce de leche means sweet of milk.
Guarapo is sugarcane juice.

At home in California, when I speak
boastful English, I can say that I fly,
but when I make the same claim in Spanish,
I have to say: *voy por avión.*
I go by airplane.

Two countries.
Two families.
Two sets of words.

Am I free to need both,
or will I always have to choose
only one way
of thinking?

FIRST FLAMES

At home in Los Angeles, when my big sister
is struck by polio, I am not yet old enough
to understand ominous words like iron lung,
quarantine, or eternal light—the candle
our *abuelita* back in Cuba
promises to ignite
in honor of La Virgen
de la Caridad del Cobre
on one condition:
that the Virgin of the Charity of Copper
will agree to spare the life
of Magdalena
Madalyn
Mad.

When Mad survives—and does not even
need a wheelchair—the joyous news travels
by telephone, all the way to the island,
where a grateful flame
begins to glow
forever.

LEARNING TO LISTEN

Dad finds a job teaching art at a college
near the Oregon border, where we will live
in a storybook house, surrounded by
a giant forest.

Mami tells me and Mad
that our new home will be
paradise, but Dad says we'll miss
his parents—my other grandma
and my grandpa, the ones who live
in Los Angeles, and don't speak any
Spanish at all, just English and Russian
and Yiddish, because they were born
in the Ukraine, a place they fled long ago,
to escape violence.

It's true that we miss them
in the northern forest, where the air
turns out to be far too cold for Mami's
tropical mind.
She dreads the fog,
hates the gloom, and fears the gray,
missing blue.

I love blue sky too, but I also love
these enormous redwood trees,
and the crashing ocean waves
on a cold rocky coast.

I love seeing green moss,
orange butterflies, blue dragonflies.
I love nature.

I also love listening
when my mother reads stories.
Her reading voice glows
with hot Cuban sun, even when
the book is in English, a language
with such strange spelling
that for her, certain sounds will always
be mysterious.

When Mami reads out loud,
all I crave is one more page,
and then another,
and the next . . .

but I'm even more fascinated
when Mami recites poetry out loud
from memory—like the one by José Martí
about growing *la rosa blanca*—the white rose—
as a gift for enemies
as well as friends.

I don't know what it means,
so Mami explains
that it's a simple verse about
forgiveness.

DANGEROUS AIR

One night,
our storybook house
in the towering forest
suddenly bursts
into flames.

Dad's paintings crumble to ash.
Mami's photos of her family in Cuba
rise into the cold sky,
stray
wisps
of
dark
smoke
blending
into gray fog.

Later, we learn that the cause of the fire
was wiring, so perfectly hidden
inside visible walls.

AFTER THE FLAMES

We move south again,
to a cabin in the foothills
of the mountains near Los Angeles,
where a sycamore tree pierces
the cabin's roof, and wild deer
behave like tame pets, sipping
from a leaky faucet.

Each night, Mami rises—silently,
secretly—to switch off all
the electricity,
so that fire
can never
find us
again.

Fear has suddenly entered our lives,
left behind by airy wisps of smoke
from those scorched
storybook walls.

MORE AND MORE HOMES

Sometimes on the weekends,
we drive to Mexico, where Dad
paints bullfights, while I stay
with a woman who has a goat
that carries me on its horns.

Later, we move to a corner
of northeast Los Angeles
known as Skunk Hollow,
because the rugged streets
are not yet paved,
so that small wild animals
roam dusty backyards.

Dad teaches art, and paints.
Mami plants flowers,
sews dresses, and listens
to old Cuban love songs,
while Mad and I roam outdoors,
searching for adventure.

MY AMERICAN DAD

Dad paints a knight on a white horse,
galloping toward a windmill.
Don Quixote, he explains—
not a real knight, just a man who dreams
of battling imaginary giants
like the windmill, with its spinning arms
and towering height.

When Dad gives me my own art supplies,
I clip a big sheet of paper onto a board,
and drape a smock over my clothes,
to keep all the colors of the world
from ruining the dress Mami made.

What should I draw, with my new
rainbow of crayons?

Dad paints my beautiful mother,
and he paints my pretty sister.
Both of them have big, dark eyes,
so why are mine blue-green-gray,
like ocean waves
in changeable
weather?

When Dad paints my portrait,
my eyes look like Don Quixote's,

neither happy nor completely sad,
just daydreamy,
and wistful.

TURTLE CAME TO SEE ME

The first story I ever write
is a bright crayon picture
of a dancing tree, the branches
tossed by island wind.

I draw myself standing beside the tree,
with a colorful parrot soaring above me,
and a magical turtle clasped in my hand,
and two yellow wings fluttering
on the proud shoulders of my ruffled
Cuban rumba dancer's
fancy dress.

In my California kindergarten class,
the teacher scolds me: REAL TREES
DON'T LOOK LIKE THAT.

It's the moment
when I first
begin to learn
that teachers
can be wrong.

They have never seen
the dancing plants
of Cuba.

WHEN I WAS A WILD HORSE

The next time I draw a picture,
it's the same gold-winged
rumba dancer, but this time
she's on horseback, smiling,
and somehow I know
that I am both
the flying rider
and the swift
steed.

After that, whenever adults
ask me if I plan to be an artist
like my father, I answer:
No, I will be
a wild horse
above green hills,
flying. . . .

MI MAMI CUBANA

On the streets of Los Angeles,
strangers ask me if my mother
is a movie star.
Her beauty makes men
turn their heads, while envious women
advise her to wear a crimson hibiscus
behind one ear, just like all the other
exotic foreign stars.

But Mami is shy.
She would rather tend a whole garden
than wear a single boastful blossom
in her dark, wavy hair.

Homesick, she listens to Cuban music.
Homesick, she sings to herself in Spanish.
Homesick, she tells stories about the island.
Homesick, she sews flowery tropical
mother-daughter dresses,
even though Mad and I prefer
to run around outdoors wearing shorts,
and never matching
at all.

When Mami gives us pretty dolls,
we toss them into a closet.
Instead, we play with insects, snails,
and earthworms.

But Mami expects us to iron bedsheets,
and set the table, while all I want to do
is read tales of adventure.

As I read *The Black Stallion*, *White Fang*,
and *The Call of the Wild*,
I notice that the heroes are always boys.
Luckily, Mami assures me
that I can do anything a boy can do.
She lets me and Mad fill our room
with living creatures.
Caterpillars, tadpoles, lizards,
stray cats and dogs, a rabbit,
and wild, wounded birds.

Mami understands us after all.
Somehow, she knows that even girls
who have to cook, clean, sew, and iron
also need the freedom to heal
injured wings.

Damaged Air

Los Angeles is smoggy.
We have to burn our trash
in a backyard incinerator.

No wonder the air feels cursed
by smoke.
No wonder Mami is still homesick
for blue sky
cleaned
by tropical storms.

One by one,
she tries a dozen arts:
developing photos in a darkroom,
spinning soft clay on a potter's wheel,
shaping hard metal into jewelry. . . .

One by one,
she masters more and more
English words, and conquers more
and more of her fears, even learning
how to drive a car, although she never
dares to try the speedy freeway.

Slowly, on side streets,
she takes us to parks with streams,
where we gather wild watercress
for bitter salads.

Still homesick, Mami finally enters
the starstruck dreams of Hollywood,
but she does not act.
No, the only role she plays is real,
her true feelings on display
as entertainment
for strangers.

The name of the ugly program
is *Queen for a Day*, a game show
where competing women cry and plead,
until one of them receives
a gold crown,
and a wish.

On TV, Mami weeps, begging
for an airplane ticket
to visit her mother
in Cuba.
But she loses.
Instead, the audience chooses
another crying woman, a blonde
who only wants a washer-dryer,
a familiar wish,
American-made,
and modern.
Metallic. Hard. Cold.
Solid.

KINSHIP

Two sets
of family stories,
one long and detailed,
about many centuries
of island ancestors, all living
on the same tropical farm . . .

The other side of the family tells stories
that are brief and vague, about violence
in the Ukraine, which Dad's parents
had to flee forever, leaving all their
loved ones
behind.

They don't even know if anyone
survived.

When Mami tells her flowery tales of Cuba,
she fills the twining words with relatives.
But when I ask my
Ukrainian-Jewish-American grandma
about her childhood in a village
near snowy Kiev,
all she reveals is a single
memory
of ice-skating
on a frozen pond.

Apparently, the length
of a grown-up's
growing-up story
is determined
by the difference
between immigration
and escape.

THE GEOGRAPHY OF LIBRARIES

Spoken stories are no longer enough
to fill my hunger.
I crave a constant supply
of written ones, too.

Each week, I check out
as many library books as I can carry,
so many that I feel like a juggler,
balancing
stacks
of entrancing
pages
in midair.

When I've finished reading
every book in the children's section,
I begin sneaking into the library's
grown-up zone, where travel books
help me dream
of islands.

OTHER JOURNEYS

Some summers,
we manage to travel,
even though Dad
has to borrow money
for visits to Cuba,
where Mami can finally see
her family, and I can feel
at home with my second self,
the invisible twin who belongs
to this wild tropical farm
instead of a modern
city.

DIFFERENT

During the school year,
there is only one of me,
a misfit bookworm
with long braids,
worried eyes,
a broken tooth
that makes me look
like a vampire,
and report cards
that I have to hide,
so I won't be
insulted
and teased.

When teachers complain that I'm bored,
they make me skip a couple of grades,
so now, overnight, I'm suddenly
so much younger
than everyone else
in a class
where I know
no one.

Now there is only one place where I can
truly belong, this endless stack
of blank pages in my mind,
an empty world
where I scribble

more and more poems,
while I walk back and forth
to my city school,
wishing
for farm life,
and a self that feels
natural.

HORSE CRAZY

Dad and Mami say that what I want
doesn't make sense—not when we live
in a busy city like Los Angeles.

They insist that I can only take art classes
and ballet, not horseback riding.

But I've read enough travel adventures
to know that, sometimes, common sense
is not something truly
worth making.

So I ride in my daydreams.
I gallop.
I fly!

EARTHBOUND

Certain summers have only huge,
flightless wings, like ostriches
or emus.

This year, my parents decide
that all we can afford is a road trip,
a long, exotic drive through hot deserts
to Mexico, where Mad and I climb
the Pyramid of the Sun
and the Pyramid of the Moon.

In tropical jungles, wild green parrots
remind me of island skies, and in villages,
I meet the pleading gazes of legless beggars
who endlessly chant *una caridad*
por el amor de Dios.
Charity, for the love of God.
Kindness.

MYSTERIES

One after another, afterlife visions
astound me.
At a village funeral,
there are festive fireworks,
and all the mourners wear white
instead of black.

Underground, in the eerie catacombs
of Guanajuato, I flee from *las momias*,
the mummies that aren't really mummies
at all, just grinning skeletons,
posed in agonized positions
that come back
in nightmares
to haunt me.

Later, along the green banks
of a quiet river in Oaxaca,
Mad and I make friends
with a boy named Pancho,
who rides his own burro,
a donkey that makes me
so envious, I can't believe
that Pancho envies me.

He thinks my city life
with cars and bicycles

must be so much more
exciting
than his donkey.

Is there any way that two people
from faraway places
can ever really
understand each other's
daydreams?

Runaway Horses

The only souvenir I want in Mexico
is a palm-leaf raincoat like Pancho's.
The dry, brown leaves feel scratchy,
but when tropical rain pours down,
I know how it feels to be a tree
that belongs to nature.

After Dad paints the stone ruins
of Monte Albán, we drive to the dreamlike
shores of Lake Pátzcuaro, in Michoacán,
where the wide nets of fishermen are shaped
like graceful
butterfly wings.

Soon, in a village on the rugged slopes
of Volcán Paricutín, we rent horses,
so we can ride up the volcano to see
a church steeple
that survived the flow
of fiery lava.

The volcano is hard and dark,
a stark landscape that makes my horse
shudder, but the sunlit church steeple
looks like something dreamed
by Don Quixote.

My frightened horse
runs away with me,
galloping
back downhill.

By the time we reach the village,
my hands are sore from clinging,
but I haven't fallen off, so I feel
as if I have absorbed
a new power,
the invisible
shadow
of courage.

HOMECOMING

By the time we cross the dusty
US border, we've spent every
centavo of borrowed travel money,
and all we have to eat
is bread with goat milk caramel,
and all I ever plan to wear
is my palm-leaf raincoat,
even though the dry fronds
are already
starting
to crumble.

NEWS

At home, I begin to suspect
that the expense of airplane tickets
was not my parents' only reason
for wandering around Mexico
all summer, earthbound,
instead of flying
through the enchanted air
to Cuba.

Revolution.
Violence.
Gunfire.
Danger.

Our old black-and-white TV flickers,
as if it has a conscience
and is reluctant
to keep showing
one horror after another.

People in Cuba are fighting.
It's a civil war to overthrow
a dictator.

Are some of Mami's many cousins
killing
others?

I wish the TV would turn
into a book with obedient pages
that could be flipped quickly
to reach the next
story.

WHAT AM I?

At school, all the teachers and students
seem angered by Cuba.
WHAT ARE YOU?
they ask.

It's a question that requires fractions,
and I don't like math.
Do I have to admit
that I'm half Cuban and half American,
or should I go even further, and explain
that Dad's parents were born in the Ukraine,
part of Soviet Russia?
Or am I just entirely American,
all the fractions left behind
by immigration from faraway nations?

WE WERE LIKE SANTA CLAUS
ON THAT POOR LITTLE ISLAND,
my teacher vows.
She kneels down and speaks directly
into my ear, as if confiding a terrible secret.
SUCH INGRATITUDE, she adds.

Clearly, it's an accusation.
Even though I don't understand,
somehow I end up
feeling guilty.

Why should such an ignorant grown-up
imagine
that she knows me?

More and More Secrets

My gentle parents, who never yell,
now spend more and more time
whispering.

I hear the sound
through solid walls.

It seems even louder
than shouting.

Even louder
than the TV news
with its conscience,
all that flickering.

SPIES

Our Skunk Hollow neighborhood
is usually friendly.

Mami knows the names of the mailman,
milkman, breadman, brushman,
knife sharpener, and Avon lady.

Mami is polite to
every door-to-door salesman,
even the ones who toss dirt
onto our floor, so they can demonstrate
vacuum cleaners.

But sometimes, friendly neighbors
become nosy.
An old woman who peeks out
from behind her curtains
loves to tell on me
if I ride my bike too fast,
or don't look both ways
before crossing the street.

When I make friends with a girl
who likes to play on the edge
of the dangerous freeway,
someone tattles, and soon
I'm in trouble.

Our neighborhood
can sometimes
turn unfriendly.

Are people staring
from behind ruffled curtains
because I'm so disobedient,
or because they know that Mami
is from Cuba?

INVESTIGATED

One day, Mami receives a phone call
that makes her look terrified.
She calls Dad and begs him to rush home.

A few minutes later, two men in suits
knock on our door.
Luckily, Dad is home by the time Mami
has to face two grim agents
from the Federal Bureau
of Investigation.
FBI.
Just like on TV.
Only somehow, now
we are suddenly
the bad guys.

What's wrong with receiving
phone calls, letters, and packages
from Cuba?

Are we supposed to care less
about Mami's family on the island
than Dad's family—my grandma
and grandpa, aunts, uncles,
and cousins
who live so close
that we see them
every Sunday?

Can one half of my family
really be so much worse
than the other?

If only I could just be myself,
instead of half puzzle
and half riddle.

AFTER THE FBI

All the magic
escapes
from the air
in our cozy home,
as if a floating balloon
has popped, leaving nothing
but a lifeless flap
of colored
plastic.

MY OWN QUESTIONS

If only I could be the one
investigating.
I would ask why the men in suits
insisted that they already have a file
for Dad, a file that could put his name
on a dreaded blacklist, so that no
museum or art gallery
will ever exhibit
his paintings.

The agents said they knew that Dad
took an art-history correspondence class
from a Communist UCLA professor
during World War II.

The agents didn't care
that when he took the class,
Dad was a sailor on an unarmed
merchant marine boat, bravely
carrying food for hungry sailors
on US Navy warships.

I have more questions than the FBI.
What is a Communist?
Who dreamed up blacklists?
How can any art class ever be
traitorous?

All I know about World War II is cruelty.
Will we be sent to prison camps,
like Jewish people in Germany,
or like our own friendly
Japanese American dentist,
who was locked away behind a tall fence,
in the California desert, right after Japan
bombed Pearl Harbor?

Why are Cubans suddenly spoken of
as enemies?
Not so long ago, Mami's island
was only known for music
and sugar.

HIDDEN

Mami moves things that came from Cuba
to the garage. Letters. Magazines.
Boxes of cookies.

Inside each box, there are surprises
the size of baseball cards—bizarre,
creepy, collectible scraps of stiff paper
that show photos of tortured men,
blood-streaked, bullet-riddled, bearded
Cuban revolutionaries, just like Mami's
cousins.

When I see her in the garage, peering
at the hideous cards, she explains
that photos are put in cookie boxes
as a form of newspaper, because
so many Cuban farmers don't know
how to read, but anyone can understand
a picture.

REFUGE

The ugliness of war photos
and the uncertainty of TV news
join the memory of FBI questions
to make me feel like climbing into
my own secret world.

Books are enchanted. Books help me travel.
Books help me breathe.

When I climb a tree, I take a book with me.
When I walk home from school, I carry
my own poems, inside my mind,
where no one else
can reach the words
that are entirely
completely
forever
mine.

THE VISITOR

My parents are brave.
They're not afraid
of the FBI.
Abuelita is coming to visit!
She's going to be right here
in our house.
We don't care if the neighbors
think Cubans are dangerous.

What will *Abuelita* think of this country?
Big freeways, huge bridges, an enormous
continent . . .

As soon as she arrives, she loves it all,
and she laughs when I admit that I'd rather
be living
on her island.

She teaches me how to embroider
a colorful bouquet of cotton flowers
that look just as cheerful as the garden
where Mami has planted a refuge
of her own, one that smells
like perfume, and is filled
with the music of bees.

How strange it seems
to be a normal family,

with two friendly grandmothers
living in the same city
at the same time.

Even though they can't speak
the same language, *Abuelita*
and Grandma
seem to understand
each other.

NO WINGS

Passports are just paper,
but without them you can't go
anywhere.

When the six-month limit
on *el pasaporte*
de abuelita
expires,
she has to return
to the island
in an airplane.

If only I had
my own
paper wings
to go with her.

REALIDAD/REALITY

Poems, travel stories, and nature
keep me hopeful.

Mad and I roam outdoors, following
the mysterious footprints of wildness—
lizards, skunks, squirrels, and birds—
that seem to carry messages
back and forth between
this dry, gravelly earth,
and the smoggy
Los Angeles sky.

Sometimes, daily life fades away,
as I wonder what my second self
would be like if we lived
on my mother's small *isla*/island
instead of my father's big *ciudad*/city.

It really is possible to feel
like two people
at the same time,
when your parents
grandparents
memories
words
come from two
different
worlds.

Winged Summer

1960

EVENING NEWS

Before all the trouble in Cuba,
Mad and I were only allowed to watch
one television program per week—
Lassie or Disney, our choice.

Now we see the news each evening.
Explosions.
Executions.
Revenge.
Refugees are fleeing from Cuba.

Mami worries about her family,
so Dad urges her to go see them.
Take the girls, he murmurs,
let's be realistic, this might be
your last chance.

Last chance? No!
I can't imagine
a future
that ends. . . .

THE LAST-CHANCE TRAIN

This summer will be so strange.
Dad won't be going with us.
Instead, he'll travel alone,
to study art in Europe.
Even though he's a teacher,
he likes to keep learning.

Mom lets us take our pet caterpillars,
but before we can soar
through the magical sky,
there is a long, rattling
three-day train trip
all the way to New Orleans.

Deserts and swamps speed past the train's
vibrating window, like weird landscapes
in a science-fiction story
about eerie planets
with fiery sunsets.
I peer into my little blue suitcase,
studying the way restless caterpillars
change into patient cocoons.

The scientific part of me knows
that I shouldn't have packed insects.
They might become farm pests
in a new place—

but who would care for them
if we left them all alone at home?

So here they are, in my luggage,
helping me understand how it feels
to slowly grow
hidden wings.

FLOWING

At the steamy train station
in New Orleans, horrifying signs
above drinking fountains
announce:
COLORED.
WHITE.

Confused, I drink out of both.
Why should it matter if a stream
of cool, refreshing water
pours
into
my
mouth
or
another?

MIDAIR

The airplane to Cuba
is nearly empty.

Are we the only people still willing
to travel in the direction of a country
that has been called troublesome
by TV newsmen?

I feel like I'm zooming
into a galaxy where everyone
is invisible, except the three of us.
Mami. Mad. Me.
And our tiny zoo
of patient cocoons.

So I stretch out on a whole row of seats,
even though the flight is short, and I am
too excited to sleep.

Turbulence shakes us.
Gusts of wind threaten to send
the plane crashing down
into deep blue water
between shorelines.

If we sink, will there be mermaids
riding sea stallions,
or sharks

with teeth
as sharp as knife blades?

Gazing down at scary waves,
I wonder if the traveling spirit
of midair magic
will wrap itself around me,
like the silky glue that ties
motionless cocoons
to dry branches.

FLUTTERING

At the airport in Havana, we step out
into the fierce heat of a tropical day.
Mad and I open our suitcases,
setting our pet butterflies free.
Yellow-and-black–striped
tiger swallowtails.
Dark mourning cloaks.
Orange viceroys.

My mind and heart start to flutter.
What have we done—will our delicate insects
find plenty of nectar, or will they starve
or grow homesick and migrate
all the way back
to California?

If only I understood
the language of wings.

REVOLUTIONARY

I remember the island as a quiet place
of peaceful horses and cows, but now
all I see are crowds of bearded soldiers
in dull green uniforms,
with dark machine guns
balanced
on rough shoulders.

The music blasting from every car radio
is a drumbeat assortment of army songs.
Speeches trumpet from bullhorns.
People whisper in small groups.
War talk.
Angry talk.
Men's talk.

Nothing to do with me, or Mad, or Mami,
or—*mira*, look, there's *Abuelita*
and my great-grandma!

WONDERSTRUCK

Dazzling flowers, cheerful trees,
colorful dresses . . .

Uniforms.
Rifles.
Beards.

While part of the stormy sky explodes
with a rumbling downpour, another area
remains peaceful and blue.
Rain and sun at the same time.
A mystery of brilliance
and darkness.

Bright parrots, festive gardens,
a rainbow . . .

Beggars.
Strangers.
Frowns.

FEELING ALMOST AT HOME

Riding in *Tío* Pepe's car, we arrive
at a small house on an unpaved road
in Los Pinos, a rural edge
of La Habana/Havana
where farms and homes
dwell in mud, side by side.

The sky is still shared between sun and rain,
but now there are vultures, too, circling
like a wheel
of darkly winged
questions.

Abuelita lives in the small house,
and my great-grandma has a bigger one
across the muddy street.

So we run back and forth,
absorbing hugs, kisses, and greetings
from dozens of curious aunts, uncles,
and cousins of all ages,
people who look familiar
and strange
at the same time.

I almost feel
like a part of me
still belongs.

LOS BARBUDOS/THE BEARDED ONES

The next day is a chance to rediscover
everything I loved when I was a baby.
Umbrella-shaped mango trees,
red-flowering flame trees,
sour *tamarindo*, with shiny seeds
that can be strung to make necklaces
shaped like brown flowers.

When a truck filled with bearded soldiers
roars down the muddy road, I'm outdoors
with Mad and a pack of roaming children—
cousins, neighbors, strangers, friends.

The soldiers chant a song about war,
a marching song that tells a story of rage
against North Americans.

Maybe I don't belong after all.
Not completely.
Not anymore.

TARANTULAS AND SCORPIONS

Questions twirl into my mind
like sudden gusts
of mixed-up fear.

How many soldiers died
in the revolution that ended
only a few months ago?

I imagine some must have been
Mami's cousins—my own relatives.
But I'm afraid to ask.
I don't want to know.

So I wander all over the farm fields
with Mad, searching for small creatures
to study, but my mind wanders too,
away from the tarantulas
and scorpions we catch—
down into deep earth,
where bones might be buried.

SECRETS

Bullets.
Coppery.
Finger-length.
Shiny.

Bullets left over from the war.
Bullets in my grandma's garden.
Are they still powerful?
Can they explode?

All the distance between dark earth
and clear air
seems to shrink.

These bullets are mine now, no matter
how forbidden.

If I don't tell any grown-ups
that I have them, I'll be safe.
Won't I?

TWO MINDS

With two bullets hidden
in the pocket of my shorts, I run
back and forth between the little house
and the bigger one.

There's hardly ever any traffic
on the muddy road, just horsemen,
singing vendors, donkeys, mules, goats,
stray dogs, and excited children.

Some of my new friends are as skinny
as skeletons.

Others own nothing
but nicknames.

Boys race and leap noisily.
Girls watch quietly.

I'm not really sure who I am anymore,
my everyday
shy bookworm
school-year
North American self . . .
or this new person,
the rogue island girl
who feels almost

as brave
as
a
boy.

My Great-Grandmother's Garden

With tangled green growth all around her,
la mamá de abuelita works as hard
as any farmer. Bananas. Papayas.
Sweet potatoes. Limes.
She can grow any food,
and smile at any joke,
even the rugged ones
told by men.

She has been alive for more
than ninety years.

She was born when Cuba still belonged
to Spain—when the island's slaves
were not yet free, and wars
were like storms, sweeping
across the farmland
every few years.

Now she plucks a sleek green fruit
from a tangled tree, and offers it to me.
This lime is the best gift I've ever received.
Fragrance. Flavor. Color. Roundness.

My great-grandma's hand looks as strong
as a garden tool, even though the skin
is papery-thin, like a daytime moon

that refuses to hide
after sunrise.

What would *la mamá de abuelita* say
if she knew about my two
hidden bullets?

What would *Abuelita* think, and Mami,
and Dad—so far away in Europe?
He was an unarmed merchant marine,
not a soldier, so wouldn't he be
disappointed in me for keeping
such a violent
secret?

I bite into the sour sweetness
of that homegrown green lime
with reverence.

The scent is a blend
of gentleness and power,
just like my great-grandma's
strong hand.

MY GREAT-GRANDMOTHER'S HAIR

At night, when *la mamá de abuelita*
frees her long, wavy white hair
from tight braids,
it flows like water,
and her years
seem to vanish.

I don't know which one of us
is time traveling.

Is she really young again,
or have I just learned how
to imagine?

STORYTELLERS

La mamá de abuelita seems easy
to please as long as I stay outdoors,
where her wild green garden
is the center
of our shared world.

But right across the street,
my sweet *abuelita* is terrified
by insects, lizards, frogs,
and spiders—she can only
keep me indoors
by telling stories about
her childhood on the farm.

As soon as my grandma stops talking,
I run back outside, where I listen
to wild stories told by grown-up cousins—
bearded men who wear olive-green uniforms
that scare me a lot more than
spiders.

MORE AND MORE STORIES

I find it hard to believe
that I am surviving
a whole summer
without a library
for finding
the familiar
old magic
of books.

But storytelling seems
like magic too—a new form
that is also
ancient
at the same time.

Will I ever be brave enough
to tell old-new tales
in my own way?

EL BOHÍO/THE HUT

In a neighbor's dirt-floored,
palm-thatched hut,
I see how few objects
some people own.

Cots, chairs, a rough table,
and a smooth, shiny saddle.
Everything here is handmade,
except for the silvery metal bit
that spins
and gleams
in a leather bridle.

No running water.
No electricity.
No car.
Just a horse—I can see him
through the open doorway,
a dark-red bay with black legs,
and a black tail and mane.
I don't have any way to know
if he's swift and heroic,
but just the sight of a horse
is enough to help me feel
like my mind is soaring
in midair, all four hooves
racing across the light
and dark
sky.

WINGS

Mami is brave.
Knowing how much
I crave horsemanship skills,
she timidly asks the neighbor
if I can ride.

The neighbor is generous, and also
amused.
He can't believe that a girl
from a country of cars
would ever care
about animals.

Mad is older, so she gets the first turn,
even though she has always claimed
that dogs are her favorite,
while I am the one who craves
amazing horses.

While my sister rides, I watch.
It looks scary.
Not easy—not smooth and graceful
like the daring chase scenes
in cowboy movies,
or those adventurous chapters
in *The Black Stallion*.

When Mad finally finishes galloping
all over the nearby fields and streets,
she reins the sweaty horse to a halt
and hops down casually so that I
can climb up
awkwardly.

Why can't I be slim and athletic,
like a racehorse jockey
or my sister?

The horse endures
my nervous efforts.
I sit too far forward,
and hold the reins
too tightly, and clench
my teeth, and clutch
the saddle horn,
first at a bumpy trot,
then a rolling canter,
and eventually,
a rapid gallop
that makes all my
daydreams
feel
real!

Airborne.
And earthbound.
At the same time.
Four hooves in the sky.
Then down again.
Winged.

SINGERS AND DANCERS

That soaring ride on a borrowed horse
was my life's dream come true.
Nothing else could ever be better,
not even the ice cream that arrives
in a mule-drawn cart.

Coconut. Pineapple. Mamey.
Tropical flavors. Colorful tastes.
When the vendor sings in praise
of the ice cream he sells,
one of Mami's teenage cousins
goes twirling out onto the street,
swirling her waist
and shaking
her
hips.

If we stay here on the island
forever, will I grow up
courageous enough
to always ride a horse
everywhere I go, and brave enough
to dance in public every time I buy
ice cream, candy, or fruit
from one of *los pregoneros*,
the singing vendors of Cuba,
who walk up and down
the streets all day,

chanting
to entrance
dancing
customers?

FIESTAS/PARTIES

My great-grandmother is livelier
than any child I've ever met.
Her house and garden are always
bursting with uncles and cousins—
bearded men and smooth-faced ones—
soldiers, farmers, a doctor, a puppeteer,
and enough neighbors to complete
any bingo, poker, or *dominó* game.

Unaccustomed to parties, I sit alone
on the quiet porch,
weaving strips of palm leaf
into miniature hats that I wear
on my fingers.

If we stay in Cuba forever,
will I learn how to chatter
and laugh, like Mami's
noisy relatives?

DOUBTS

Mami is having
some sort of problem
with her passport.

If she doesn't receive an exit visa—
permission to leave Cuba—
and an entry visa—
permission to reenter the United States—
then we might not be allowed
to fly home in time to meet Dad
when he returns to California
at the end of summer.

Maybe this island is not
a source of courage after all,
because suddenly
Mami looks terribly anxious
instead of wonderfully brave.

LA GUAGUA/THE BUS

We ride a crowded *guagua*
all the way to downtown La Habana,
where there are government offices
with answers for people
who have complicated,
two-country,
mixed-family
questions.

La guagua only stops for old women,
little girls, and pretty ladies like Mami.
Men and boys have to run, leap, and grab
any part of the bus they can catch.
They have to hang on, while women
and girls
sit on the seats
and relax.

I've always envied boys, whose lives
seem so much more adventurous,
but the truth is that right now,
I don't really mind having a restful place
beside a smudged window
where I can press my nose
against the glass,
gaze out,
and feel
safe.

EXPLORATION

On certain mornings, Mami grows
so busy with her passport troubles
that Mad and I forget to worry,
especially when all three of us
are invited on day trips
in *Tío* Pepe's car.

A beach where flying fish
leap and soar.

A jungle with enormous flowers
that look like bright red
lobster claws.

Waterfalls and lagoons,
quiet pools of swirling
blue.

Farms, villages, towns . . .
this island is an endless adventure
as we speed from place to place
in a car. . . .

So why am I still so envious
every time I see a village child
on horseback or riding
in an oxcart?

Some of the sights
that Mami describes
as dire poverty
look like such
luxurious wealth
to a city girl
who loves
farms.

TRAVELING TO MY MOTHER'S HOMETOWN

We're finally leaving La Habana
behind!

We're on our way to Mami's
hometown of Trinidad de Cuba,
on the island's south coast,
where my parents met.

It's only half a day away,
but even though I've been there before,
it seems like a journey through centuries,
slow and dreamlike, completely old,
yet strangely new.

As we pass sugarcane fields
and banana plantations,
everything turns emerald green,
as if we're headed toward Oz.
But there will be no wizards
in Mami's hometown,
just more relatives, and the house
where she grew up, and the farm
where both *Abuelita*
and my great-grandma
were born.
The farm where I
plan to turn into
my real self.

Quiet Times

I feel like I'm home,
even though this peaceful town
isn't my own.

Everything is just as I remember
from before the war.
Palm trees and bell towers rise
above rows of houses, each wall
painted its own shade of fruit hue.
Guava pink. Lime green.
Pineapple yellow.

A whole town just as quiet
and colorful
as a garden.

Blue doves flutter from nests
on the red tile roofs.
Horsemen lead goats
along cobblestone lanes.

We stay in a house
where I don't remember all the names
of Mami's relatives, but I do recall
the comfort of cool tile floors
on bare feet.

Immediately, old folks start scolding me
for ignoring the luxury
of shoes.

Mami explains that in Cuba
there are worms that can creep in
through the soles of your feet
and then eat their way up
to your heart.

How can any place
so peaceful
be so dangerous?

TROPICAL WINDOWS

In this centuries-old house,
each floor-to-ceiling window
is truly an opening—no glass,
just twisted wrought iron bars
that let the sea breeze flow in
like a friendly spirit.

At night, fireflies blink inside rooms,
and big, pale green luna moths float
like graceful wisps of moonlight.

In the morning, all those night creatures
vanish, replaced by cousins and neighbors
who peer in through the barred windows
to greet me and chat.

When *Tío* Darío brings sugarcane
from the farm, I chew the sweet stems,
absorbing a flavor that tastes
like beams of sunlight.

Is it okay to pretend
that everything will always be easy?
No passport troubles for Mami.
No courage questions for me.
No bullets.
No worms.
No death.

Just open windows, hot sunlight,
and winged creatures that fly
in and out.

LA SIESTA/THE NAP

After a big lunch of yellow rice
and black beans, all the grown-ups
fall asleep in rocking chairs.

Children are expected to rest
at siesta hour, but Mad and I know
that this is our best chance
to explore.

The central patio has fruit trees
and flowers to study, and the walls
display intriguing old black-and-white
photos of ancestors, wide-eyed pictures
that make me feel
just as drowsy
as a grown-up,
all filled up
with years.

LOST IN TRANSLATION

One day, we walk along the cobblestones
to visit a sick relative who is so old
that I'm surprised by her strength
as she pinches my arm and sighs,
¡Ay, que gordita! How chubby.

I know that I'm a tiny bit pudgy,
but being called fatty by a grown-up
makes me cry so long and so hard
that all Mami's efforts to explain
are useless.

I don't care if plump is a compliment
in Cuba. I can't stand the sight of this old
skinny, sick woman, who envies anyone
healthy enough to gain weight.

Why can't an insult contain only
one meaning, so that I can hate her,
even if she might be dying?

ESCAPE

Living in between two ways
of speaking
and hearing
makes me feel as divided
as the gaps between
languages.

At least we're finally
on our way to the farm,
where there will be more animals
than people, and I won't have to struggle
to understand
old folks.

As we bump along a muddy track
in *Tío* Darío's battered jeep, I inhale
the scent of roadside flowers
that grow tall and weedy,
rooted in mud
the color of blood.

Red soil.
Green hills.
White cows.
Horses of so many shades
that the colors can't be
counted.

Everything looks just as wild and free
as I've half-remembered
and half-imagined.

It's as if my other self has been here
all along—
the invisible twin
who never left this island
and never
will.

GUAJIROS/FARMERS

The shower is a bucket.
The bathroom is an outhouse.

Dinner is a piglet—cute and squealing,
until one of the older cousins
has to slit its throat and dig a pit
and roast the meat
in a nest of stinky garlic
and sour orange juice,
on a bed of slippery
green banana leaves,
underground,
just like
a grave.

Maybe I'm not brave enough
to be a real farm girl
after all.

SEPARATION

Mami is leaving us here.
It will be my first time spending
a whole night far away from her.

She says she's going to see
more relatives, and visit a beach
and a beautiful cave.

I can't help but wonder
if there's also something mysterious
that has to be asked and answered
in one of those government offices
where powerful strangers
make decisions about the passports
of people who belong to mixed-up,
two-country, complicated
families.

El Rodeo/The Roundup

With Mami gone, Mad and I are eager
to help with farm chores,
but we don't like helping the women,
who do nothing interesting—
just cook, sew, sweep, and wipe
the noses and bottoms of babies.

We want to ride with the boy cousins,
rounding up white cows each evening,
so that they can be milked
in the morning.

Mad is allowed to help with *el rodeo*,
because she's older and a better rider,
but I have to wait my turn.

Tío Darío promises that there will be plenty
of other summers when I can ride, rope,
and be brave, like a boy.

WAITING MY TURN

That night, I sleep
in the farmhouse,
listening to owls,
mosquitoes,
and cows.

Listening
to horses.
My future.

The Milking Hour

Dawn on the farm means rising
before the sun to rush outdoors
into a corral where men and older boys
milk the cows, while cats prowl,
waiting for their chance to sip
spilled droplets.

I hold a clear glass under an udder,
letting it catch a creamy stream
of warm froth
that tastes
like moonlight.

By the end of next summer,
I'll be older.

Maybe by then, I'll finally be allowed
to learn the magic
of milking.

RITMO/RHYTHM

Mad has decided to catch a vulture,
the biggest bird she can find.

She is so determined, and so inventive,
that by stringing together a rickety trap
of ropes and sticks, she creates
a puzzling structure that just might
be clever enough to trick a buzzard,
once the trap's baited with leftover pork
from supper.

Mad and I used to do everything together,
but now I need a project all my own,
so I roam the green fields,
finding bones.

The skull of a wild boar.
The jawbone of a mule.

Older cousins show me
how to shake the mule's *quijada*,
to make the blunt teeth
rattle.

Guitars.
Drums.
Gourds.
Sticks.

A cow bell.
A washboard.
Pretty soon, we have
a whole orchestra.

On Cuban farms, even death
can turn into
music.

NEVER ENDING

Up there, the law does not reach,
a secretive cousin whispers,
pointing toward the jungled peaks
of tall green mountains.

The war isn't over after all.
Some of the revolutionaries
have turned into
counterrevolutionaries.
Men who fought together
now fight against one another.

What if the battles
go on and on
forever?

My Grandmother's Mare

Men with machetes chop sugarcane.
Boys on horseback show off rope tricks.
I'll never get tired of seeing
all the things I don't know
how to do.

The one thing I know best
is how to daydream
while watching horses,
so when *Tío* Darío
points to a red mare
with a round belly,
and tells me that she belongs
to his sister—my *abuelita*—
I ask if I can ride her.

Not yet, is the frustrating answer.
But the mare is pregnant,
and my great-uncle promises
that next summer, I can help
train the foal, which,
according to *Tío* Darío
will be
half mine!

I'll be expected to share with my sister,
but in just a few short months,
each of us will be half owner

of a colt
or a filly.

When I squeeze the sun-browned hand
of my grandma's brother, his skin feels
as hard as a tree trunk,
scarred by farmwork
and strengthened by time.

Next summer—so soon,
but my excitement makes a whole year
seem
like forever.

BREATH

Today all the cousins are riding
out to a thicket of wild *mamoncillo* trees,
where even the girls will be allowed to climb
up tall trunks to pick fruit, and bring back
enough for the grown-ups.

One of the older boys leads me
to a brown horse that has no saddle,
just a small, square patch of blanket
that shifts around as I climb up a fence
to make myself tall enough for a leap
onto the back of the gelding that will
carry me fast enough to catch up
with Mad and all the cousins,
who are already
so far ahead. . . .

Across a field, up a hill, and then—
so soon, before I've even had a chance
to prove my courage—the scrap
of blanket slips backward, sliding
off the rump of the horse, so that I
tumble into a swamp of muddy red
hoofprints.

The horse stops, turns, and gazes at me,
perplexed, his dark eyes asking why
I was foolish enough to mount him

with just a blanket, instead of a tightly
cinched saddle, and the sturdy
reassurance of stirrups.

How will I ever manage to train
a spirited young colt or filly
if I can't even ride an old gelding?

I wipe my tears, and this time, I climb up
onto the horse's bare back
without the help of a fence, leaving
that slippery blanket
where it belongs, half-buried
in blood-red mud, while I cling
to the thick mane with both hands,
and grasp strong brown sides
with my legs.

I can feel the hot air
steaming from horse sweat,
a smell that will always
remind me of courage.

By the time I reach distant fruit trees,
the harvest is over, all the cousins
wheeling their horses around
to ride home.

It doesn't matter, because
with exhilarated breath
and a drumming heart,
I feel as if I've galloped
so far beyond anything
I've ever known before
that I'm already grown-up
and independent.

HASTA PRONTO/UNTIL SOON

I came to this island of relatives
with nothing but butterflies.

Now I'm leaving with secret bullets,
and a gleaming, pale yellow stalactite
that Mami brought from a cave
where Cuban Indians
hid from Spanish invaders.

I have a wild boar's skull, too,
and the rattling jawbone
of a musical mule,
and the promise
of a horse to share
with my sister.
A filly or colt of our own,
next summer's
treasure.
Soon.
So soon.

Strange Sky

1961–1964

THE FARAWAY GIFT

Back in the United States, I return to quiet days
of reading and schoolwork and waiting
for a letter from *Abuelita*.

When it arrives, a small photo
of a chestnut colt
is enclosed inside a folded sheet
of airmail paper
so delicate
that it resembles
a sliver
of moonlight.

Long legs. Bristly mane.
The red colt looks wild,
like a prehistoric horse.
Mythical. Prophetic.
An oracle colt who foresees
my future as a trainer,
adventurer,
explorer—
maybe even a winged
centaur.

Next summer,
the transformation
will begin!

Until then,
my true self
awaits me in Cuba.

Until Next Summer

I'll have to share the red colt with Mad,
but some treasures are so stunning
that fantasies about them
become private.

It's the same way
when I think of boys,
who used to look
like nothing more
than short, boring,
grown-up men.

Now they're beginning to seem
mysterious, even though I'm only
nine, and most boys still
ignore me.

OUT OF REACH

News from the island grows worse
each day.
Diplomats are expelled.
Relations between the two countries
I love
break down.

Dad says there won't be a next summer
on the island.
No visit, no farm life, no horse,
no winged centaur.

No *Abuelita* either,
or Great-Grandma.

Mami turns into Mom, changing
before my eyes
from an ordinary person
who left her homeland
believing that she would return
every year—
to this strange, in-between-nations
exile, a lost wanderer
whose country of birth
and extended family
suddenly seem
as remote
as the moon
or Mars.

SOME THINGS SHOULD NEVER CHANGE

I know exactly when Mami became Mom,
but Dad is still Dad, painting Don Quixote,
the wistful knight who dreams of courage.

The eyes of those paintings
still look like my eyes.

How long will it be
until the two countries I love
forgive each other and move on
so that I can live on horseback,
like that wistful knight,
the dreamer?

I'm not even sure what there is to forgive.
Something about Cuba seizing ownership
of oil refineries.
It's all so confusing.
Why should something as ugly as oil
affect friendships between nations?

WHY DO WE HAVE TO MOVE?

I love to travel, but I hate moving.
Dad wants an art studio, and Mom
longs for a bigger garden,
so they've borrowed money
to buy a strange house
on a steep hill,
a precarious home
that feels dangerous,
as if it could slide
down this slope
during the next
earthquake.

Mom struggles to tame
her fierce hillside garden
of poisonous castor bean weeds
and intriguing trap-door spiders—
clever, big-eyed creatures who peer
from small, round doorways,
the entrances to dark,
hidden tunnels
deep in this dry clay soil
of our oddly wild
city home.

STRAYS

Sixth grade in a new school
means a long hike down the steep hill
on a wooden stairway that takes the place
of a street, as if I have moved
into a story about some other
century.

Mad has already started junior high,
and the girl next door calls me Spanish
and treats me like a curiosity,
so I feel completely alone
at this new school
where no one knows me.

Hardly anyone speaks to me,
until one day
on the way home,
I find a tiny calico cat
stranded beneath
the wooden stairway.

The colorful stray kitten
offers me the poetry
of her purr,
so I pick her up,
take her home,
and demand
the right
to keep her.

My parents are so distracted by news
that they say yes, even though
Dad is allergic and Mad has
a new puppy.

My kitten will have to be an outdoor cat,
but that's fine, because I want to stay
outdoors too, playing all day
with bugs and plants
instead of people.

I have no human friends, and no way
to reach the island of my horse,
so I search for birds and blossoms
to identify, and I carry a hammer,
just in case I find rocks with crystals
or fossils to extract.

There's something about knowing
the names and faces
of nature's creations
that helps me feel
almost at home
in my sharply divided
shrinking
world.

MY LIBRARY LIFE

Books become my refuge.
Reading keeps me hopeful.
I fall in love with small poems,
the shorter the better—haiku
from Japan, and tiny rhymes
by Emily Dickinson.

Then I move on to long volumes
that I can't really understand—sonnets
and plays by Shakespeare, and novels
written for adults—tales of tropical lands
with a hot, brilliant sun that shines down
on human troubles.

Things Fall Apart by Chinua Achebe
from Nigeria.
Nectar in a Sieve by Kamala Markandaya
from India.

I never find any books
about the beautiful green
crocodile-shaped island
that throbs
at the center of my being,
like a living creature,
half heart
and half beast.

Maybe someday
I'll try
to write one.

APRIL 1961

Bay of Pigs.
A swampy invasion.
It's all over the news—
an attack by CIA-trained
Cuban exiles, armed
with weapons
from the United States.

They landed only fifty miles from Trinidad.
But they're soon defeated.
The vast United States loses,
while tiny Cuba wins, and now
both governments
are even angrier
than before.

Travel restrictions are tightened.
There's no way we'll ever
be able to visit the faraway half
of our family.

Junior High

A stay-at-home summer
of books, spiders, a kitten,
plants, rocks, and then, in September:
Washington Irving Junior High.
A school named for the author
of *The Legend of Sleepy Hollow*.
Maybe that's why I feel
like a shadow.

Seventh grade.
Eleven years old.
A bookworm-misfit
with long black braids,
childish white socks,
pointy pink glasses,
and no courage
for flirting.

It doesn't take long to learn
that I'm ridiculous.

Girls ignore me, or tell me to cut
my old-country braids,
while boys ignore me, or taunt me
for wearing thick glasses.

So I stumble through the halls—
glassesless—enduring blurry vision

in my doomed effort
to fit in.

By the end of the first month,
I've chopped off my hair
and started ratting it,
thrashing the black strands
backward,
to create stiff
knots and tangles.

I shave my legs.
Experiment with eyeliner.
Mascara.
Lipstick.

A rolled-up skirt
serves as a dare, inviting
the stern girls' vice principal
to suspend me.

She does.
One whole afternoon at home
with a book.

If only I could change
my timid nature,
instead of my
short skirt.

LEARNING

Once I've mastered the art
of pretending that I don't care
what other kids think of me,
I start to pay attention in class,
discovering that I love
library research
for history term papers
about ancient lands.
It feels like a form
of time travel.

In English class, I write myths—
stories to explain small
scientific mysteries,
such as why does a sloth
hang upside down,
and how does a snail
feel about time?

At home, I scribble tiny poems
all over the walls of my room.
Inside those miniature verses,
I feel safe, as if I am a turtle,
and the words
are my shell.

LEARNING THE HARD WAY

I love words, but I hate numbers.
In algebra, bizarre formulas defeat me.
I don't care why X is greater than Y.
I don't even care if I flunk.
There's no point working so hard,
when other kids mock me anyway,
for being smart, while feeling stupid.

So I ditch class to hide in the bathroom,
pretending to smoke.

Girls who really do smoke stare at me.
Gradually, they begin talking to me.
One by one, they appear to befriend me,
asking—will I write their term papers?
Will I do their English and history homework?
Sure.
Why not?
I'm already in trouble.
Why not hang out with troublemakers?

SOLITUDE

So I join other girls who belong
nowhere, and we roam together
at school.

But on weekends,
while they go to parties,
I walk alone to a museum
where Native American weaving
and baskets are on display.
Unsigned.
Unclaimed.
I'll never know the names
of the women who made
all these beautiful objects
of useful art.

Does the work of a girl
always have to be
so anonymous?

OCTOBER 1962

Grim news.
Chilling news.
Terrifying.
Horrifying.
Deadly.

Just the shock and fear are enough
to make old people die of heart attacks,
while young ones have to endure
a vigil, this torment,
the slow wait
to start breathing
poisoned air.

US spy planes have photographed
Soviet Russian nuclear weapons
in Cuba.

Air-raid drills at school.
Doomsday warnings.

Rants against the island.
Hate talk.
War talk.
Sorrow.
Rage.

SOLITARY

I feel like the last survivor
of an ancient tribe,
the only girl in the world
who understands
her language.

This huge city feels too small
to hold all my feelings.
I crave a true wilderness,
where I can be alone.
Unknown.

My parents must be in shock,
because they mostly speak
to each other, and mostly
in whispers.

I imagine they must be saying things
too terrible for me and Mad
to hear.

MORE DANGEROUS AIR

Newsmen call it the Cuban Missile Crisis.
Teachers say it's the end of the world.

At school, they instruct us to look up
and watch the Cuban-cursed sky.
Search for a streak of light.
Listen for a piercing shriek,
the whistle that will warn us
as poisonous A-bombs
zoom close.

Hide under a desk.
Pretend that furniture is enough
to protect us against perilous flames.
Radiation. Contamination. Toxic breath.

Each air-raid drill is sheer terror,
but some of the city kids giggle.
They don't believe that death
is real.

They've never touched a bullet,
or seen a vulture, or made music
by shaking
the jawbone
of a mule.

When I hide under my frail school desk,
my heart grows as rough and brittle
as the slab of wood
that fails to protect me
from reality's
gloom.

WAITING TO DIE

Nearly two weeks of horror.
Anger. Dread. Visions of doom.
From October 22 to 28,
no one speaks of anything
but mushroom clouds.
Atomic bombs.
Cuba.
Evil.

Supermarket shelves are empty.
Food and water are hoarded.
Gas masks are stored in bomb shelters—
expensive underground chambers
that only rich people can afford.

The rest of us will be left aboveground,
where we'll have to inhale
poisoned air.

WAITING TO UNDERSTAND

At home, silence.
At school, chatter.

During visits to Dad's relatives,
long, complicated arguments
about Communism.
Capitalism.
War.
Peace.
Survival.

I escape to Aunt Marcella's
quiet den, where I read magazines
and adventure books,
instead of listening
to grown-up
confusion.

WAITING TO BE RESCUED

US Navy warships surround the island.
Talks between leaders are the only hope.
Secret talks.
Mysterious talks.
All I know is whatever I learn
by listening as TV newsmen
struggle to guess, trying to predict
the horrifying
future.

Powerful messages must be
passing back and forth
between the American president
and the Soviet premier.
Kennedy.
Khrushchev.

The whole world's safety depends
on the words of two men
who are enemies.

WONDERING

I don't understand Communism
or capitalism, or presidents
or premiers, or nuclear
radiation.

I do know that *aire* means both
spirit and air.
Breath.
Inhalations.
Dangerous.
Precious.

How will I decide whether to breathe
toxic sky?

And what about an afterlife?
Is there anything beyond this slow torment
of waiting to die?

IMAGINING

My sister tells me the plots
of horror movies, while our parents
watch more and more news.

I don't know which is worse,
The Blob and *13 Ghosts*,
or NBC and CBS.

I can hardly stand either one.
All I want to do is read
The Iliad and *The Odyssey*,
Aesop's Fables, *The Tempest*,
A Midsummer Night's Dream.
Ancient tales with endings
that have meanings
instead of doubts.

SURVIVAL

Diplomacy succeeds. Words win.
Death loses.

At the end of two weeks of secret talks
by world leaders,
the rest of the earth's people can finally
breathe.

Nations were not destroyed.
Cities were not devastated.
No one died.

It wasn't a real war.
Newsmen spoke of the Cold War,
an almost-war of words,
not a battle of bombs
and blood.

It's safe to inhale now.
No radiation.

No poison.
Except for the toxins
left behind in teachers' minds
when they talk
about Cuba.

THREE SIDES TO EVERY STORY

Two world powers in the Cold War
make me think of the two forms
of enchantment in fairy tales.

One is helpful, the other dangerous.
The first we call magic, the other
an evil spell.

But what about Cuba?
If the United States is all good,
and Soviet Russia is all bad,
then what is the island,
and how did it feel to be trapped,
like *Abuelita* and my great-grandma,
Tío Pepe, *Tío* Darío, the cousins?

Trapped between Russian missiles
and North American warships.

Surrounded.
No borders to cross.
No way to escape.
All around, in every direction,
just blue sea and blue air,
all the beauty and danger
of natural water
and powerful sky.

And what about afterward?
Will *Abuelita* be expected
to think of us
as her enemy?

LIFE GOES ON

Days and nights are once again
strangely normal.

School. Daydreams. Books.
Wall-poems. Family.

Then, my first junior high dance.
Boys are shy.
Girls are disappointed.

Later, at my first junior high party,
in a house where the parents
aren't home, hardly anyone is timid.
Almost everyone drinks, smokes, laughs,
and makes out.
Except me.

I am still only
eleven.

FIRST

First kiss.
On a pier.
At the beach.
He's sixteen.
I'm eleven.

I could vow
that I love him
or claim
that I hate him.

All I know
is a first kiss
should not be
like this.

So I run.
Away.
Alone.
Confused.

LAST

After I race away from that scary
first kiss, I have no hope for love,
or even like.

No more childhood
or in-between dreams.
Nothing to think of
as my future.

No real self.
Just books.

The only goal in junior high seems to be
finding a boyfriend, but all I have now
are disappearing friends—older girls
who brag about weed, meth, heroin,
sex, and other adventures
that have nothing
to do with me.

Soon, most of my new friends
are pregnant and addicted.

They drop out of school,
leave their parents' houses,
apply for welfare.

When I see them at the mall,
pushing babies in strollers,
they look old and tired.

REBELLION

I argue with my parents
about nothing important.

I cut up travel magazines,
and cover the poem-free spaces
on all my bedroom walls
with bright pictures
of sunny places.

I feel old enough to travel
on my own,
ready to flee
and leave home.

So I begin to save
all my babysitting money
for a journey—alone—
to India or Fiji or Brazil,
any place tropical
and distant.

INVISIBLE

Why don't we ever talk about Cuba
anymore?

No one at home or school
seems to remember the Missile Crisis
and the Cold War.

The island has vanished from maps
in travel magazines, from posters
at travel agencies, from books
in history class.

No one wants to think about
those two weeks of fear
that almost killed us.

Does my invisible twin still exist
over there, the brave island girl
who knew how to dance
and gallop?

SMALL JOURNEYS

We never really travel
as a family anymore,
not beyond US borders.

All our adventures are short
and simple.

Local mountains. Trickling streams.
Together, we sit beside the flow
of gentle water, listening.

Dad wants to go back to Europe,
to study a new art technique,
but Mom is stateless now.

Without any diplomatic relations
between the United States and Cuba,
there is no embassy or consulate.
No place to renew her expired
passport.

CLOSE TO HOME

News is all about the United States now.
Mississippi. Memphis. Martin Luther King Jr.
When an Alabama church is bombed
by racist extremists, four girls are killed,
civil rights workers are murdered,
people all over the country
march to demand equal rights.

My family marches too.
My own off-key voice rises, singing
"We Shall Overcome," and other songs too,
about being like a tree standing by water,
refusing to move.

Soon, I think of my life as bigger and bolder
than junior high.

But when President Kennedy
is assassinated, newsmen are quick
to blame Cuba.

GHOSTLY

Mom stays home
from the marches.

What if she's still being watched
by the FBI?
Could they deport her?

She could change her country.
Take a naturalization test.
Answer all the questions.
Swear allegiance to the United States.
Become a citizen.
Vote.
Face facts,
accept the loss of her right to travel
back and forth to the land
of her birth.
But she won't.

Everything else about her island
seems so distant
that she clings
to her useless
passport—that last
papery link.

I've heard stateless people
referred to as ghosts.

No identification.
No country.
They can't cross borders.
But most of them are refugees,
who have no chance to choose
a new country.

Is Mom the only person on earth
who remains
ghostly
by choice?

COMMUNICATION

Cuba starts to seem real again.
Abuelita writes letters in code,
inventing poetic metaphors,
to prevent the island's censors
from understanding her words.

When she says that *Tío* Darío
is working hard in the garden,
Mom somehow knows that it means
he's been arrested, and sent
to a prison or a forced labor camp.
We don't know why—did he give food
to those counterrevolutionaries
fighting in the mountains?
Did they drink fresh milk
and chew sweet sugarcane
from emerald-green fields?

Other news is just as shocking.
Singing vendors are outlawed.

Selling anything is illegal.
No one is allowed to make a profit.

Religions will soon be outlawed too.
What will happen to the eternal flame

that *Abuelita* ignited when Mad
survived polio
so long ago?

WILDERNESS

When another summer comes,
we escape from the confusion
of city life and world news
and personal loss
by camping.

We hike beside waterfalls,
climb a rounded mountain,
and rent gentle horses
to ride
on wild trails.

It's the closest we've come
in a long time
to feeling
like a normal
family.

REVIVED

At home, Mom starts a hospital
for abandoned and neglected
house plants, pulling them
out of our neighbors'
plastic trash cans.

She nurses the roots back to health
with water, fertilizer,
and hope.

Her efforts are rewarded
with spectacular blossoms.

Watching her, I learn
how to help lost things
spring
back to life.

Two Wings

1965

A SWIRL OF CHANGES

Some lost things can be brought back to life,
but others have to be transformed.

Mad and I listen to the Beatles,
while Dad insists on opera,
and Mom still chooses romantic
boleros, and lively *son montuno,*
the music of *guajiros* who ride horses
and drive oxcarts.

Certain ideas begin to flow backward
from young to old.
Mad and I teach Mom to stop
ironing sheets, start wearing jeans,
and give up speaking so politely
that she can't explain the birds
and bees
of teenage life.

When she tries to teach us about dating,
they're rules she learned
when she was a girl:
Never call boys.
Wait to be asked.
When an invitation
finally arrives,
don't act too eager.

Why do I always feel like I'm waiting
for my real life
to start?

Travel Plans

With new words like "hippie"
suddenly replacing "beatnik"
and "bohemian," Dad reclaims
the wanderlust
of his youth.

England, France, Italy,
and a whole month in Spain.
He's borrowed enough money
for six months in Europe, where he
will study a new art technique
in Paris, and then, in the summer,
we'll join him
to roam like nomads.

But only if Mom can obtain
special permission by visiting
all sorts of government agencies.

Her plans have to be precise.
Dates and ports of entry
for each country
must be officially approved
in advance.
It's the same
for departures.
No nation wants to risk
a visit from a stateless
Cuban ghost.

REALITY

Mom is nervous. Anxious. Fearful.
She speaks to her rescued plants,
urging brown leaves
to turn green.

Our new travel plans are so real,
while memories of Cuba seem
imaginary.

But the island is not a fantasy.
Poetic letters from *Abuelita* reveal pain.
The farm is gone, confiscated.
Cattle, horses, and cousins
have vanished.
Food is rationed.
Cubans are hungry.

But at school, we don't study
our own nation's trade embargo
against the island.

Teachers no longer mention
the travel ban or the Missile Crisis
or statelessness
or refugees
or the future.

All we learn about is ancient Rome
and George Washington,
as if only the distant past
can ever be
understood.

MY OWN VIEW OF HISTORY

Cold War.
My icy
dread.

Cold War.
My frozen
hopes.

But how can an almost-war,
or anything else, remain frozen for long,
on such a hot tropical island
where even the coolest
sea breeze
feels
steamy?

SOARING

Flying over Ireland,
the rolling green hills
make me think of Cuba.

In London, I'm held spellbound
by the gracefully arched neck
of a white marble horse,
carved
and galloping.

In France, each cathedral offers
art lessons from Dad, but along with
the spectacular light and dramatic
architecture, each brilliant
stained glass window
contains a story.
Desert. Savior. Angels.
Shepherds. Pilgrims. Saints.
Beggars. Suffering.
Hope.

NOMADIC

Gargoyles.
Castles with dungeons.
Winding roads that lead us
from village
to village.

We are a family of wanderers.
Every meal is a picnic of fresh bread,
apples, yogurt, and cheese.

I no longer feel sullen and sad.
On the road, I am free to be
child-hearted again, filled with wonder,
a daring explorer, unafraid of seeing
new places, unusual people,
strange customs,
odd ways. . . .

CAVE PAINTINGS

In Spain, we venture underground,
into the mystery of prehistoric art.
Bison, horses, human handprints.
Herds of wild feelings
long extinct.

The cavern walls are cool stone,
covered with earthy pigments
of red, brown, and yellow clay.

Shapes in the ancient stone
become the swollen bellies
and curved horns
of painted animals.

The herds seem to move,
rippling through time.

I begin to understand
that each time I scribble
a poem on my wall
at home, I am not really
alone.

Certain longings
are shared
by all.

Even cavemen.
Cavewomen.
Children.
Teens.

IMAGINARY HORSES

When we reach the wheat fields
of La Mancha—the part of Spain
where a storybook dreamer
imagined that he was a brave knight—
Dad becomes unusually playful,
bursting with delight
at the chance to experience
the land of Don Quixote,
the subject of so many
of his own wistful paintings.

Dad seizes a stick to use as a lance,
and places a bowl upside down
on his head to create a helmet
that gives him the courage
to attack a windmill, as he pretends
that the slowly spinning blades
are the enormous arms
of a monstrous
giant.

Watching an artist who believes
in the power of stories,
I find it easy
to see
the puffing breath
of a brave knight's
invisible horse.

Secret Languages

All over Spain, strangers speak to us
in Spanish, then whisper to one another
in forbidden dialects—Basque, Catalán,
and Gallego, all the banned tongues
of local provinces.

The words are illegal,
outlawed
by a dictator.

I notice the fearful way
Spaniards glance
at uniformed officers
of the Guardia Civil.

Could they actually be arrested
just for whispering ordinary words?

I've never had to live in a place
where I would not be allowed to speak
all my opinions
openly.

Now I imagine how it must feel
to really *need* poetic metaphors,
instead of just enjoying
their simple beauty.

No wonder *Abuelita* always finds
such flowery ways of saying ugly things
in her carefully censored
airmail letters.

By now, I am old enough to understand
that the island's revolution merely replaced
one tyranny with another.

Right wing or left wing, tyrants always
try to control communication.
They always
fail.

VILLAGE LIFE

After we visit many cities and see
each amazing art museum, we settle
for a month in a rented house
on a sunny hill, above a rocky beach.

When the village celebrates a festival,
young men let cows chase them
off the end of a pier.
Even though the cows
make the strong young men look silly,
laughter helps everyone feel
united.

When nomadic *gitano*/Gypsy caravans
pass across the land in horse-drawn wagons,
I feel like every creature on earth
just might be mysteriously linked,
as we wander from one place
to another, constantly learning
about one another's ways.

UNANSWERABLE QUESTIONS

Unable to swim skillfully, I watch Mad
and Dad as they have fun in the waves.
Why have they always been so brave
in daily life, while Mom is only courageous
in strange ways, and I am only bold
with words?

The villagers are friendly and talkative,
even though they complain to me
about the United States, asking why we
support their dictator, and why we
build US Air Force bases in Spain.
I don't know how to answer questions
about governments.
Not mine.
Not theirs.
Certainly not Cuba's.

All I know is that I'm grateful
for my two languages,
so that I can explain
that I can't explain.

Speaking almost feels
like having
wings.

FINAL FLAMES

When a heat wave
brings a wildfire,
sweeping swiftly
down a hillside,
all the villagers
line up to pass
buckets of water
from hand to hand,
working together
to prevent
devastation.

It's a sight I plan to remember,
this spontaneous unity
when faced
with disaster.

MY SECOND WING

Poetry feels like one wing
of my mind's ability to travel
away from gloom.

Now, Spain has reminded me
that other journeys
are magical too.
I can love
many countries,
not just two.

Moving on after a month
in the village, we visit the houses
of famous artists in France and Italy,
where we see marble statues
and magnificent paintings.

But mixed with those adventures,
there is one stark moment
that stays with me—ghostly—
after we're turned away
from the Swiss border
simply because
Mom's passport is Cuban.
By the time we leave Europe,
I'm fourteen, with gold loops
in my ears, like the Gypsies,

and exotic stamps
all over my passport.

My passport.
The disturbing document
that specifically states
it cannot be used for travel
to Cuba.

HOPE

All I know about the future
is that it will be beautiful.

An almost-war
can't last
forever.

Someday, surely I'll be free
to return to the island of all my childhood
dreams.

Normal diplomatic relations.
An ordinary family—united.
Magical travel, back and forth.
It will happen.
When?

Cold War Time Line

The following list shows only a few of the most easily understood events of a complex and perilous era when much of the world was divided into hostile regions.

1945
The United States destroys the Japanese cities of Hiroshima and Nagasaki with the world's first military use of nuclear weapons.

After World War II, the Allies divide Germany into US and Russian–influenced zones of occupation.

1948
Communist takeover of Czechoslovakia launches a long series of Soviet military actions in Eastern European nations.

1949
Soviet Russia detonates its first nuclear weapons.
Communist revolution in China.

1950–1953
Korean War; Korea is divided into Communist and capitalist zones.

1954
US-armed overthrow of the democratically elected government in Guatemala launches a long series of American military actions in Latin American nations.

1956–1959
Revolution in Cuba.

1960
Cuba nationalizes oil refineries and many other American-owned
businesses on the island; the United States restricts trade with
Cuba; Cuba increases trade with the Soviet Union.

1961
US-trained Cuban exiles attack the island in the failed Bay of Pigs
Invasion; Cuba's government aligns with the Soviet Union; the
United States breaks diplomatic relations with Cuba and restricts
travel by American citizens.

The German Democractic Republic (Communist East Germany)
government builds the Berlin Wall to stop its citizens from fleeing
to US influenced West Germany.

1962
The "Cuban" Missile Crisis (known in Cuba as the October
Crisis, and in Russia as the Caribbean Crisis) results when Russian
nuclear weapons on the island are detected by US spy planes; the
entire world hovers on the brink of all-out atomic war until the
crisis is resolved through secret negotiations between US president
Kennedy and Soviet premier Khrushchev; Russian missiles are
withdrawn from Cuba in exchange for the withdrawal of US
missiles from Turkey; US travel restrictions are tightened.

1965–1975
Vietnam War—the United States is defeated.

1979–1989
Soviet war in Afghanistan—Russia is defeated.

The Berlin Wall is deactivated and pulled down.

The Soviet Union crumbles after Eastern European nations declare independence.

1991
Worldwide end of the Cold War, with the exception of ongoing tensions between North and South Korea, and continued US travel and trade restrictions against Cuba.

2014
Simultaneous announcements by US president Barack Obama and Cuban leader Raúl Castro, declaring that a gradual process of normalizing diplomatic relations, trade, and travel will begin in January 2015.

Author's Note

Enchanted Air is the true story of my first fourteen years. Since early memories tend to swirl through time, certain events are undoubtedly out of order, while others probably entered my mind through stories told by older relatives, or even by looking at photographs.

I never thought I would be brave enough to write about my life as a Cuban American child growing up in the United States during the hostilities of the Cold War. I thought it would be too excruciating. That is why I have chosen to focus on travel memories. Travel is a magical experience. Travel opens the heart and challenges the mind. Travel gives us an opportunity to see how others live, whether they are relatives or strangers. Travel teaches compassion.

Soon after my last childhood visit to Cuba in 1960, a devastating travel ban was imposed by the United States Treasury Department, under the Trading with the Enemies Act. While I was still a teenager, I began applying for permission to return to Cuba. With visas denied by both countries, I pushed the island to the back of my mind. Eventually, my grandmother became a refugee. Both she and my mother became US citizens.

As an adult, I studied agriculture, botany, and creative writing, became the first woman agronomy professor at one of California's polytechnic universities, and traveled all over Latin America, eager to learn about other countries. I married, raised a family, and enjoyed an ordinary North American life, but that sense of loss left by the Cold War—an almost-war—never passed.

In 1991, thirty-one years after my last childhood visit to my mother's homeland, I was finally blessed with a chance to visit relatives, who began calling me the family's ambassador. More than half a century after the Missile Crisis, the two countries I love had not yet renewed diplomatic relations. I have returned to Cuba many times with humanitarian-aid programs and for legal family visits, but as I write this, one of the closest neighbors of the United States is just beginning to be accessible to other American citizens.

While I was writing *Enchanted Air*, my hope was that normalization would begin before it went to press. That prayer has been answered. May this little book of childhood memories serve as one of José Martí's white roses—a poetic plea for the chance to treat neighbors like friends.

Margarita Engle
January 2015

Cultivo una rosa blanca,
en julio como en enero,
para el amigo sincero
que me da su mano franca.

Y para el cruel que me arranca
el corazón con que vivo,
cardo ni oruga cultivo;
cultivo la rosa blanca.

I grow a white rose,
in July, as in January,
for the sincere friend
who gives me his honest hand.

And for the cruel one who rips out
the heart with which I live,
I don't grow thistles or weeds;
I grow the white rose.

—José Martí
from *Versos Sencillos (Simple Verses)*

ACKNOWLEDGMENTS

I thank God for the magic of travel and the miracle of hope.

I am profoundly grateful to my parents, sister, and extended family for childhood travel experiences, and to my husband and children for later journeys.

Abrazos a los primos.

For suggesting that I write a childhood memoir, I am eternally grateful to Oralia Garza de Cortes.

Hugs to the following friends who listened as I moaned about the difficulty of writing a childhood memoir: Sandra Ríos Balderrama, Angelica Carpenter, and Joan Schoettler.

Special thanks to my wonderful agent, Michelle Humphrey, my amazing editor, Reka Simonsen, and the entire fantastic publishing team at Atheneum. For the stunning jacket art, I am grateful to Edel Rodriguez, and for a beautiful design, I am thankful to Debra Sfetsios-Conover.